The Old-Fas
THANK YOU
POSTCARD BOOK

Martin Greif

A Sterling/Main Street Book
Sterling Publishing Co., Inc.   New York

10 9 8 7 6 5 4 3

A Sterling/Main Street Book

Copyright © 1992 by Sterling Publishing
Published by Sterling Publishing Company, Inc.
387 Park Avenue South, New York, N.Y. 10016
Distributed in Canada by Sterling Publishing
c/o Canadian Manda Group, P.O. Box 920, Station U
Toronto, Ontario, Canada M8Z 5P9
Distributed in Great Britain and Europe by Cassell PLC
Villiers House, 41/47 Strand, London WC2N 5JE, England
Distributed in Australia by Capricorn Ltd.
P.O. Box 665, Lane Cove, NSW 2066

Manufactured in Hong Kong
All rights reserved

ISBN 0–8069–8451–1

The act of saying "thank you" has long been seen as more than just a common courtesy. The Roman statesman Cicero wrote that "gratitude is not only the greatest of virtues, but the parent of all the others," a sentiment echoed and amplified in the lovely old French proverb, "Gratitude is the memory of the heart." Anticipating by well over two millennia the social grace of voicing formal thanks for kindesses shown, and for doing so without delay, an unknown Greek writer reminded us that "swift gratitude is sweetest; if it delays, all gratitude is empty and unworthy of the name."

Although the practice of writing formal thank you notes is as ancient as the art of writing itself, the sending of preprinted greeting cards to express one's thanks is a relatively recent tradition. The first commercial thank you cards, in fact, date only from the early twentieth century, during the height of the picture postcard craze. All the thank you cards reprinted in this book originally appeared between 1907 and 1914, the years between the Federal Governments's decision to permit handwritten messages to appear on the address side of a penny postcard and the decline of the postcard industry after the introduction of greeting cards with envelopes. At the zenith of the picture postcard's popularity (1913), Americans bought some 968 million cards.

The golden age of postcard art comes alive in *The*

Old-Fashioned Thank You Postcard Book. Each card, printed in its original vibrant colors on heavy mailing stock, is perforated for easy removal. And each card provides ample space on the reverse side for the sender's personal wishes. At a cost of less than 25¢ each, these period postcards are not only a greeting card bargain, but an imaginative and tasteful example of the cardmaker's art suitable for the most deserving recipient.

Most of the postcards in this book were supplied by Don and Newly Preziosi, dealers in vintage postcards and paper. Information about their holdings in a large number of postcard collecting categories can be had by writing Preziosi Postcards, Box 498, Mendham, New Jersey 07945, or by calling (201) 543-4721.

Thank You

SER. 523

Sincere Thanks

From *The Old-Fashioned Thank You Postcard Book* © by Sterling Publishing Co., Inc.

From *The Old-Fashioned Thank You Postcard Book* © by Sterling Publishing Co., Inc.

Thank You

SER. 523

Sincere Thanks

Post Card

Thank You

It was Jolly Good Fun!

Thank You

573.

Thank You!

It was Jolly Good Fun!

Thank You

Post Card

Sincere Thanks

Thank You...
I'm Moved to Tears

From *The Old-Fashioned Thank You Postcard Book* © by Sterling Publishing Co., Inc.

From *The Old-Fashioned Thank You Postcard Book* © by Sterling Publishing Co., Inc.

Post Card

From *The Old-Fashioned Thank You Postcard Book* © by Sterling Publishing Co., Inc.

Thank You

Sincere Thanks

From *The Old-Fashioned Thank You Postcard Book* © by Sterling Publishing Co., Inc.

From *The Old-Fashioned Thank You Postcard Book* © by Sterling Publishing Co., Inc.

Thank You

Sincere Thanks

Post Card

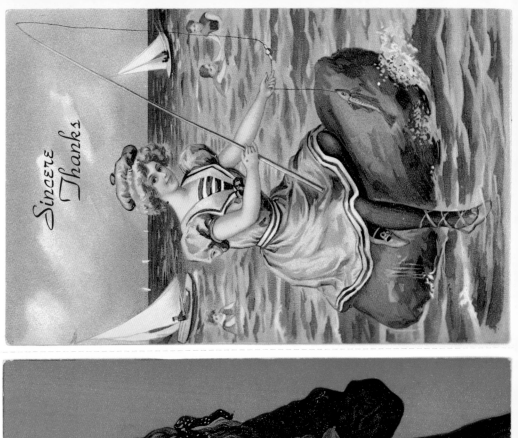

Sincere Thanks

Thank You

Thank You

Sincere Thanks

Post Card

Thank You

Sincere Thanks

Thank You

My Thanks to You

SER. 801

Post Card

Sincere Thanks

Thank You

Sincere Thanks

Serie XVI. „Lied der Liebe". Verlag Rafael Neubet, Wien VII. Nachdruck verboten.

E. Döcker jun

Thank You

Greetings
and
Sincere Thanks

JUST·A· GREETING FROM

Sincere
Thanks

My Thanks to You

Thank You

From *The Old-Fashioned Thank You Postcard Book* © by Sterling Publishing Co., Inc.

From *The Old-Fashioned Thank You Postcard Book* © by Sterling Publishing Co., Inc.

Thank You...

Sincere Thanks...

Meissner & Buch Leipzig Künstler-Postkarten Serie 1243. Wer mich lieb hat, holt mich weg. Gesetzl. geschützt.

Kindest Regards
and Sincere Thanks

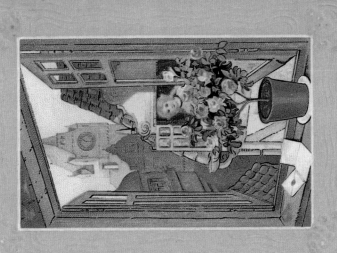

Best Wishes
and Sincere Thanks

Post Card

Sincere Thanks

Thank You!
It was Jolly Good Fun!

Post Card

From *The Old-Fashioned Thank You Postcard Book* © by Sterling Publishing Co., Inc.

Send charming and beautifully designed cards throughout the year!

The Old-Fashioned Birthday Postcard Book
The Old-Fashioned Christmas Postcard Book
The Old-Fashioned Christmas for Kids Postcard Book
The Old-Fashioned Congratulations Postcard Book
The Old-Fashioned Get Well Postcard Book
The Old-Fashioned Happy Anniversary Postcard Book
The Old-Fashioned Holiday Postcard Book
The Old-Fashioned Love & Friendship Postcard Book
The Old-Fashioned Party Invitation Postcard Book
The Old-Fashioned Thank You Postcard Book
The Old-Fashioned Thinking of You Postcard Book

Filled with classic art from rare, turn-of-the-century originals, each book has 40 full-color, ready-to-mail postcards. They're a wonderful alternative to expensive commercial greeting cards. They're also a simple way to send thoughtful and tastefully designed cards throughout the year. Both friends and loved ones will cherish these unique examples of the cardmaker's art from the past.

 **A Sterling/Main Street Book**
Sterling Publishing Co., Inc.   New York